Zachary TAYLOR

Heidi M.D. Elston

Big Buddy Books
An Imprint of Abdo Publishing
abdopublishing.com

abdopublishing.com

Published by Abdo Publishing, a division of ABDO, PO Box 398166, Minneapolis, Minnesota 55439.
Copyright © 2017 by Abdo Consulting Group, Inc. International copyrights reserved in all countries. No
part of this book may be reproduced in any form without written permission from the publisher. Big Buddy
Books™ is a trademark and logo of Abdo Publishing.

Printed in the United States of America, North Mankato, Minnesota
062016
092016

THIS BOOK CONTAINS
RECYCLED MATERIALS

Design: Sarah DeYoung, Mighty Media, Inc.
Production: Mighty Media, Inc.
Editor: Rebecca Felix
Cover Photographs: Getty Images
Interior Photographs: Corbis (pp. 5, 21); Getty Images (pp. 9, 27); North Wind (pp. 15, 17, 19);
    Picture History (pp. 6, 7, 11, 13, 23, 25, 29)

Cataloging-in-Publication Data

Names: Elston, Heidi M.D., author.
Title: Zachary Taylor / by Heidi M.D. Elston.
Description: Minneapolis, MN : Abdo Publishing, [2017] | Series: United States
    presidents | Includes bibliographical references and index.
Identifiers: LCCN 2015957560 | ISBN 9781680781182 (lib. bdg.) |
    ISBN 9781680775389 (ebook)
Subjects: LCSH: Taylor, Zachary, 1784-1850--Juvenile literature. | Presidents--
    United States--Biography--Juvenile literature. | United States--Politics and
    government--1849-1850--Juvenile literature.
Classification: DDC 973.6 [B]--dc23
LC record available at http://lccn.loc.gov/2015957560

Contents

Zachary Taylor

Zachary Taylor was the twelfth US president. He was the first person without previous **political** experience to become president. Taylor was elected president in 1848.

At this time, the United States was growing. Americans were arguing over slavery. Taylor owned slaves. But, he did not believe new states should allow slavery.

Southerners wanted slavery allowed in new states. The South began talking about leaving the United States. Taylor worked to prevent this.

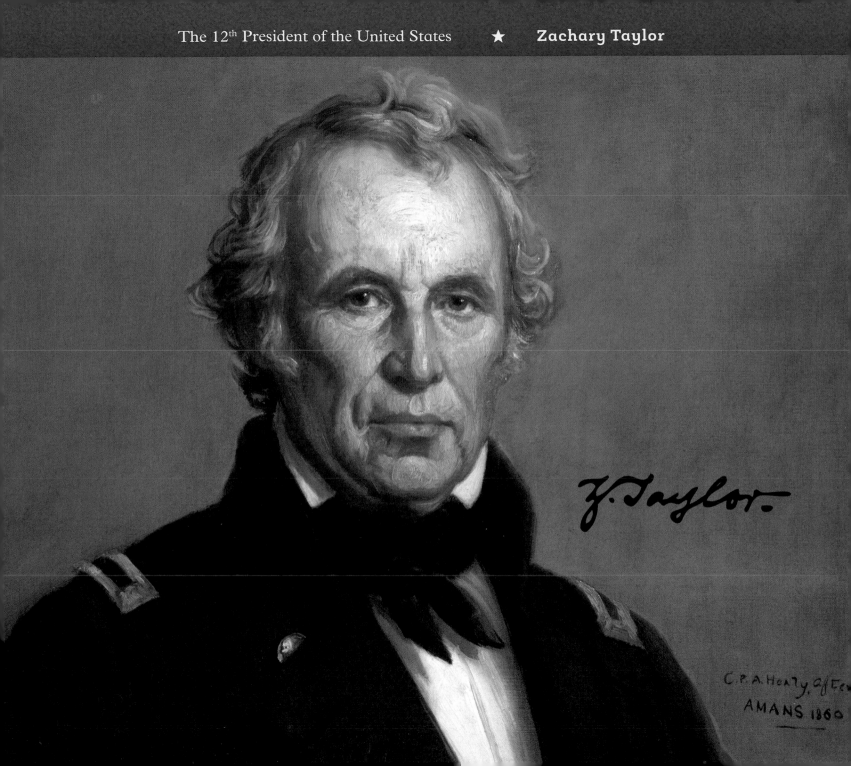

Timeline

1784

On November 24, Zachary Taylor was born in Orange County, Virginia.

1819

Taylor became a lieutenant colonel.

1808

Taylor joined the US Army as a first **lieutenant**.

1840

Taylor became the commander at Fort Smith in Arkansas.

1849

On March 5, Taylor became the twelfth US president.

1848

Taylor was **nominated** to run for president.

1850

Zachary Taylor died on July 9.

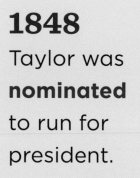

Young Zachary

Zachary Taylor was born in Orange County, Virginia, on November 24, 1784. He had five brothers and three sisters.

In 1785, the Taylors moved to what is now northern Kentucky. There, Zachary grew up on a **plantation** in Jefferson County.

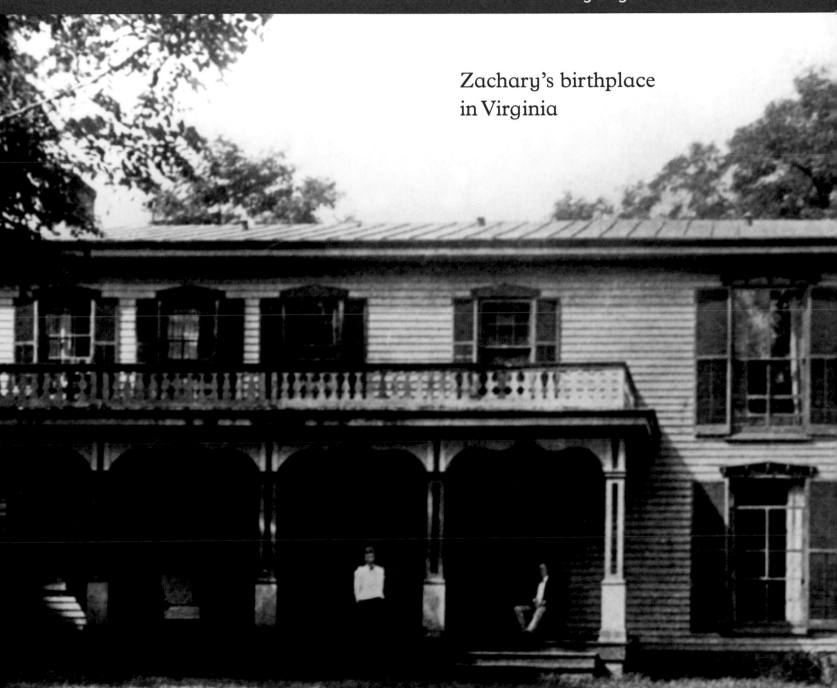

Zachary's birthplace
in Virginia

Military Family

In 1808, Taylor joined the US Army. He was a first **lieutenant**. Taylor became a captain in 1810.

That same year, Taylor met and married Margaret Mackall Smith. The couple had five daughters and one son. Two daughters, Octavia and Margaret, died very young.

The Taylors' three remaining daughters were Sarah, Ann, and Mary Elizabeth. All three women married military men. And the Taylors' son, Richard, served in the military.

Richard Taylor
served as a
lieutenant
general.

A Great War Hero

During the **War of 1812**, Taylor served at **frontier** posts in Indiana Territory. He soon became a major. Then in 1819, Taylor became a **lieutenant** colonel.

Taylor was a respected military leader. He often placed himself close to enemy fire. Taylor's men nicknamed him "Old Rough and Ready."

In 1840, Taylor became commander at Fort Smith in Arkansas. He later commanded Fort Jesup in Louisiana. Taylor's home was in Baton Rouge, Louisiana.

Old Rough
and Ready
and his horse,
Old Whitey

War with Mexico

Meanwhile, **tension** was growing between the United States and Mexico. In 1845, the United States **annexed** Texas and made it a state. This angered Mexico.

Then, the two countries disagreed about Texas's southwestern border. Both nations prepared for war. In 1846, President James K. Polk sent General Taylor to Texas.

The **Mexican-American War** began on May 13. Taylor and his soldiers entered Mexico. They took the city of Monterrey on September 24.

The capture
of Monterrey

In 1847, President Polk decided to move an army to Veracruz. From there, the United States would attack Mexico City.

Polk ordered many of Taylor's men to move to this new position. The Mexican army learned of the US plans. It decided to attack Taylor at Buena Vista.

Taylor's army won the battle! The win made Taylor an American hero. Mexican and American leaders signed a peace **treaty** on February 2, 1848.

At Buena Vista, Taylor's army numbered about 5,000 men. Still, they won even though Mexico had between 16,000 and 20,000 troops.

Getting Elected

In 1847, Taylor returned to his Louisiana **plantation**. The 1848 US presidential election approached. Many Americans thought Taylor should run for president.

Taylor was not interested in seeking election. He was happy to stay home and farm. But Taylor agreed to run if the **nomination** was offered to him.

The **Whig Party** nominated Taylor to run for president. Millard Fillmore of New York was chosen as his **running mate**.

Taylor's running mate, Millard Fillmore, served in Congress from 1833 to 1835. He served again from 1837 to 1843.

During the campaign, slavery was an important topic. Taylor rarely spoke about his views on slavery. However, he owned more than 100 slaves. This appealed to many Southern voters. Northern voters liked Taylor's military record.

Taylor promised that his **administration** would include people from all over America. In November 1848, Americans voted. Taylor and Fillmore won the election!

★ DID YOU KNOW? ★

The 1848 presidential election made US history. For the first time, all states voted at the same time.

A Taylor campaign banner

FOR PRESIDENT OF THE PEOPLE

ZACHARY TAYLOR

About party creeds let party zealots fight
He cant be wrong whose life is in the right. —

President Taylor

On March 5, 1849, Taylor was **inaugurated**. As president, his greatest accomplishment was in **foreign** affairs. The United States wanted to build a **canal** across Nicaragua. The waterway would connect the Atlantic and Pacific oceans.

Great Britain was also interested in building a canal. Great Britain and the United States arranged an important **treaty**. Both agreed to keep the canal **neutral** once it was built.

Normally, Taylor would have taken office on March 4. However, he did not want to be inaugurated on a Sunday, so he took office the next day.

Slavery Problem

Once he took office, Taylor voiced his views on slavery. He believed Southerners should be allowed to keep their slaves. But, he also believed new states should not allow slavery.

In 1849, California wanted to join the United States as a free state. Taylor **supported** this. But some Southerners wanted slavery in California.

Southerners were not happy. Some wanted the South to become a new, separate country. President Taylor did not want this. He promised to use force to keep the country together.

PRESIDENT TAYLOR'S CABINET

March 5, 1849–July 9, 1850

★ **STATE:** John M. Clayton
★ **TREASURY:** William Morris Meredith
★ **WAR:** George Washington Crawford
★ **NAVY:** William Ballard Preston
★ **ATTORNEY GENERAL:** Reverdy Johnson
★ **INTERIOR:** Thomas Ewing (from March 8, 1849)

Taylor (*center*)
and his cabinet

Many congressmen thought of ways to solve the slavery problem. Senator Henry Clay of Kentucky was one. In 1850, Clay shared his ideas with Congress.

Clay thought some new states should allow slavery. President Taylor did not **support** this. He stood firm against new slave states.

Northerners and Southerners continued to argue. The congressmen who supported Clay's **compromise** would win. However, this would not happen while Taylor was in office.

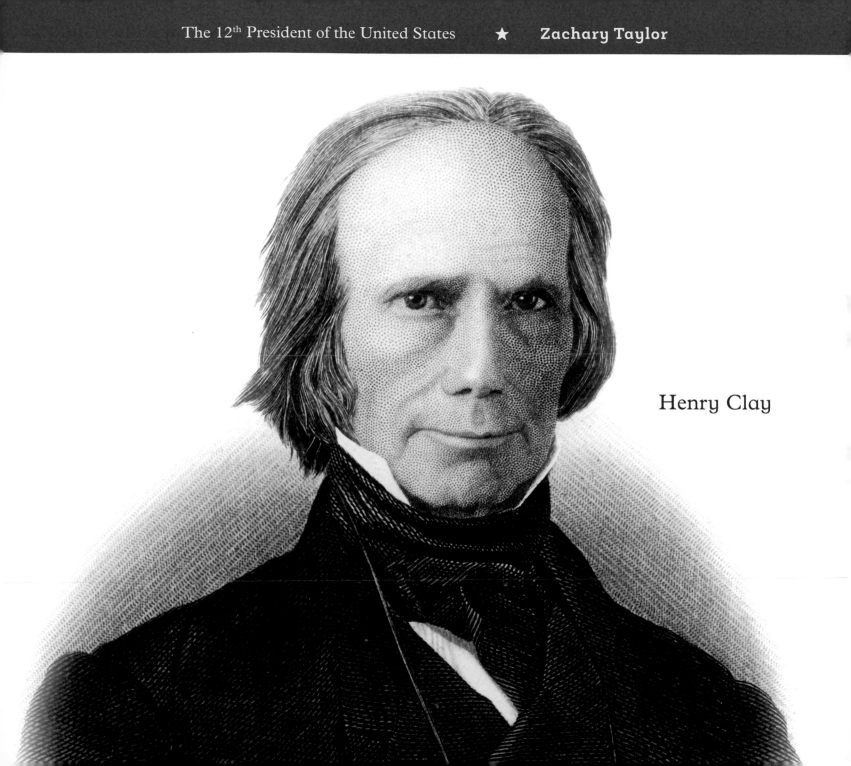

Henry Clay

A Sudden Death

On July 4, 1850, President Taylor became sick. He stayed in bed for five days, but he did not improve. On July 9, President Zachary Taylor died. He was buried near Louisville, Kentucky.

Taylor was in office for only 16 months. But he served his country for more than 40 years as a military leader. As president, Zachary Taylor fought to **maintain** the United States of America that he loved.

Taylor was the second president to die in office. He is buried in the Zachary Taylor National Cemetery.

Office of the President

Branches of Government

The US government has three branches. They are the executive, legislative, and judicial branches. Each branch has some power over the others. This is called a system of checks and balances.

★ Executive Branch

The executive branch enforces laws. It is made up of the president, the vice president, and the president's cabinet. The president represents the United States around the world. He or she also signs bills into law and leads the military.

★ Legislative Branch

The legislative branch makes laws, maintains the military, and regulates trade. It also has the power to declare war. This branch includes the Senate and the House of Representatives. Together, these two houses form Congress.

★ Judicial Branch

The judicial branch interprets laws. It is made up of district courts, courts of appeals, and the Supreme Court. District courts try cases. Sometimes people disagree with a trial's outcome. Then he or she may appeal. If a court of appeals supports the ruling, a person may appeal to the Supreme Court.

Qualifications for Office

To be president, a candidate must be at least 35 years old. The person must be a natural-born US citizen. He or she must also have lived in the United States for at least 14 years.

Electoral College

The US presidential election is an indirect election. Voters from each state choose electors. These electors represent their state in the Electoral College. Each elector has one electoral vote. Electors cast their vote for the candidate with the highest number of votes from people in their state. A candidate must receive the majority of Electoral College votes to win.

Term of Office

Each president may be elected to two four-year terms. The presidential election is held on the Tuesday after the first Monday in November. The president is sworn in on January 20 of the following year. At that time, he or she takes the oath of office.
It states:

> I do solemnly swear (or affirm) that I will faithfully execute the office of President of the United States, and will to the best of my ability, preserve, protect and defend the Constitution of the United States.

31

Line of Succession

The Presidential Succession Act of 1947 states who becomes president if the president cannot serve. The vice president is first in the line. Next are the Speaker of the House and the President Pro Tempore of the Senate. It may happen that none of these individuals is able to serve. Then the office falls to the president's cabinet members. They would take office in the order in which each department was created:

Secretary of State

Secretary of the Treasury

Secretary of Defense

Attorney General

Secretary of the Interior

Secretary of Agriculture

Secretary of Commerce

Secretary of Labor

Secretary of Health and Human Services

Secretary of Housing and Urban Development

Secretary of Transportation

Secretary of Energy

Secretary of Education

Secretary of Veterans Affairs

Secretary of Homeland Security

Benefits

★ While in office, the president receives a salary. It is $400,000 per year. He or she lives in the White House. The president also has 24-hour Secret Service protection.

★ The president may travel on a Boeing 747 jet. This special jet is called Air Force One. It can hold 70 passengers. It has kitchens, a dining room, sleeping areas, and more. Air Force One can fly halfway around the world before needing to refuel. It can even refuel in flight!

★ When the president travels by car, he or she uses Cadillac One. It is a Cadillac Deville that has been modified. The car has heavy armor and communications systems. The president may even take Cadillac One along when visiting other countries.

★ The president also travels on a helicopter. It is called Marine One. It may also be taken along when the president visits other countries.

★ Sometimes the president needs to get away with family and friends. Camp David is the official presidential retreat. It is located in Maryland. The US Navy maintains the retreat. The US Marine Corps keeps it secure. The camp offers swimming, tennis, golf, and hiking.

★ When the president leaves office, he or she receives lifetime Secret Service protection. He or she also receives a yearly pension of $203,700. The former president also receives money for office space, supplies, and staff.

PRESIDENTS AND THEIR TERMS

PRESIDENT	PARTY	TOOK OFFICE	LEFT OFFICE	TERMS SERVED	VICE PRESIDENT
George Washington	None	April 30, 1789	March 4, 1797	Two	John Adams
John Adams	Federalist	March 4, 1797	March 4, 1801	One	Thomas Jefferson
Thomas Jefferson	Democratic-Republican	March 4, 1801	March 4, 1809	Two	Aaron Burr, George Clinton
James Madison	Democratic-Republican	March 4, 1809	March 4, 1817	Two	George Clinton, Elbridge Gerry
James Monroe	Democratic-Republican	March 4, 1817	March 4, 1825	Two	Daniel D. Tompkins
John Quincy Adams	Democratic-Republican	March 4, 1825	March 4, 1829	One	John C. Calhoun
Andrew Jackson	Democrat	March 4, 1829	March 4, 1837	Two	John C. Calhoun, Martin Van Buren
Martin Van Buren	Democrat	March 4, 1837	March 4, 1841	One	Richard M. Johnson
William H. Harrison	Whig	March 4, 1841	April 4, 1841	Died During First Term	John Tyler
John Tyler	Whig	April 6, 1841	March 4, 1845	Completed Harrison's Term	Office Vacant
James K. Polk	Democrat	March 4, 1845	March 4, 1849	One	George M. Dallas
Zachary Taylor	Whig	March 5, 1849	July 9, 1850	Died During First Term	Millard Fillmore

PRESIDENT	PARTY	TOOK OFFICE	LEFT OFFICE	TERMS SERVED	VICE PRESIDENT
Millard Fillmore	Whig	July 10, 1850	March 4, 1853	Completed Taylor's Term	Office Vacant
Franklin Pierce	Democrat	March 4, 1853	March 4, 1857	One	William R.D. King
James Buchanan	Democrat	March 4, 1857	March 4, 1861	One	John C. Breckinridge
Abraham Lincoln	Republican	March 4, 1861	April 15, 1865	Served One Term, Died During Second Term	Hannibal Hamlin, Andrew Johnson
Andrew Johnson	Democrat	April 15, 1865	March 4, 1869	Completed Lincoln's Second Term	Office Vacant
Ulysses S. Grant	Republican	March 4, 1869	March 4, 1877	Two	Schuyler Colfax, Henry Wilson
Rutherford B. Hayes	Republican	March 3, 1877	March 4, 1881	One	William A. Wheeler
James A. Garfield	Republican	March 4, 1881	September 19, 1881	Died During First Term	Chester Arthur
Chester Arthur	Republican	September 20, 1881	March 4, 1885	Completed Garfield's Term	Office Vacant
Grover Cleveland	Democrat	March 4, 1885	March 4, 1889	One	Thomas A. Hendricks
Benjamin Harrison	Republican	March 4, 1889	March 4, 1893	One	Levi P. Morton
Grover Cleveland	Democrat	March 4, 1893	March 4, 1897	One	Adlai E. Stevenson
William McKinley	Republican	March 4, 1897	September 14, 1901	Served One Term, Died During Second Term	Garret A. Hobart, Theodore Roosevelt

PRESIDENT	PARTY	TOOK OFFICE	LEFT OFFICE	TERMS SERVED	VICE PRESIDENT
Theodore Roosevelt	Republican	September 14, 1901	March 4, 1909	Completed McKinley's Second Term, Served One Term	Office Vacant, Charles Fairbanks
William Taft	Republican	March 4, 1909	March 4, 1913	One	James S. Sherman
Woodrow Wilson	Democrat	March 4, 1913	March 4, 1921	Two	Thomas R. Marshall
Warren G. Harding	Republican	March 4, 1921	August 2, 1923	Died During First Term	Calvin Coolidge
Calvin Coolidge	Republican	August 3, 1923	March 4, 1929	Completed Harding's Term, Served One Term	Office Vacant, Charles Dawes
Herbert Hoover	Republican	March 4, 1929	March 4, 1933	One	Charles Curtis
Franklin D. Roosevelt	Democrat	March 4, 1933	April 12, 1945	Served Three Terms, Died During Fourth Term	John Nance Garner, Henry A. Wallace, Harry S. Truman
Harry S. Truman	Democrat	April 12, 1945	January 20, 1953	Completed Roosevelt's Fourth Term, Served One Term	Office Vacant, Alben Barkley
Dwight D. Eisenhower	Republican	January 20, 1953	January 20, 1961	Two	Richard Nixon
John F. Kennedy	Democrat	January 20, 1961	November 22, 1963	Died During First Term	Lyndon B. Johnson
Lyndon B. Johnson	Democrat	November 22, 1963	January 20, 1969	Completed Kennedy's Term, Served One Term	Office Vacant, Hubert H. Humphrey
Richard Nixon	Republican	January 20, 1969	August 9, 1974	Completed First Term, Resigned During Second Term	Spiro T. Agnew, Gerald Ford

PRESIDENT	PARTY	TOOK OFFICE	LEFT OFFICE	TERMS SERVED	VICE PRESIDENT
Gerald Ford	Republican	August 9, 1974	January 20, 1977	Completed Nixon's Second Term	Nelson A. Rockefeller
Jimmy Carter	Democrat	January 20, 1977	January 20, 1981	One	Walter Mondale
Ronald Reagan	Republican	January 20, 1981	January 20, 1989	Two	George H.W. Bush
George H.W. Bush	Republican	January 20, 1989	January 20, 1993	One	Dan Quayle
Bill Clinton	Democrat	January 20, 1993	January 20, 2001	Two	Al Gore
George W. Bush	Republican	January 20, 2001	January 20, 2009	Two	Dick Cheney
Barack Obama	Democrat	January 20, 2009	January 20, 2017	Two	Joe Biden

"I am conscious that the position which I have been called to fill, though sufficient to satisfy the loftiest ambition, is surrounded by fearful responsibilities." Zachary Taylor

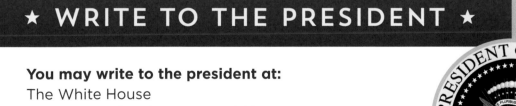

★ WRITE TO THE PRESIDENT ★

You may write to the president at:
The White House
1600 Pennsylvania Avenue NW
Washington, DC 20500

You may e-mail the president at:
comments@whitehouse.gov

Glossary

administration (uhd-mih-nuh-STRAY-shuhn)—a group of people that manages an operation, a department, or an office. An administrator is a person who works as part of an administration.

annex—to take land and add it to a nation.

canal—a channel dug across land to connect two bodies of water so ships can pass through.

compromise—an agreement reached after each side gives up something.

foreign—located outside one's own country.

frontier—the edge of settled land, where unsettled land begins.

inaugurate—to swear into a political office.

lieutenant—an officer of low rank in the armed forces.

maintain—to keep something in an existing state or in good condition.

Mexican-American War—a war between the United States and Mexico that lasted from 1846 to 1848.

neutral—not taking sides in a war or disagreement.

nominate—to name as a possible winner.

plantation—a large farm.

politics—the art or science of government. Something referring to politics is political. A person who is active in politics is a politician.

running mate—someone running for vice president with another person running for president in an election.

support—to believe in or be in favor of something.

tension—a state of unfriendliness or disagreement between individuals or groups.

treaty—an agreement made between two or more groups.

War of 1812—a war between the United States and England from 1812 to 1815.

Whig Party—a US political party active between 1834 and 1854.

★ WEBSITES ★

To learn more about the US Presidents, visit **booklinks.abdopublishing.com**. These links are routinely monitored and updated to provide the most current information available.

Index